MOONSNOOP

Written by Jill Atkins
Illustrated by Angie Sage

Heinemann

Andrew Groom is a boy
Too cool to be true!
He invented a Moonsnoop
From plans that he drew.

Sister Sue said, 'I like it!
Let's make it today!
We can find lots of things
In the shed where we play.'

They found cardboard boxes,
A boot and some glue,
An old broom, a bent spoon,
And a spare fuse box too.

They fixed the old broom
To the box and the boot.
They found an old hooter
That went, 'Toot, toot, toot!'

‘We can paint it bright blue,
Then add a red hoop.
We’ll zoom up,’ said Andrew,
‘And soon loop the loop.’

Andrew said, 'I'm the Captain
And I need a crew.'
Sue said, 'I am Captain!
We'll have to have two!'

They put on their space suits
And big space boots too.
'Are you ready?' asked Andrew.
'*I'm* Captain!' said Sue.

They started the Moonsnoop.
'Let's see if it flies.'
The blue sparks that flew
Gave them both a surprise.

'Vroom, vroom,' went the Moonsnoop,
Zooming high in the sky.
Sue tooted the hooter
As stars scooted by.

They saw planets and comets
As they raced on their way.
When the moon came in view,
Sue said, 'Let's land and play!'

Andrew pulled the broom lever.
Sue pushed the bent spoon.
And they made a crash landing
On top of the moon.

Dust flew up as they landed
Deep down in the gloom.
They were in a huge crater
By a tall tree in bloom.

They peered from the crater.
'Look out!' shouted Sue.
'We're Moonbeeps,' beeped the Moonbeeps.
'We're pleased to meet you.'

Sue gave them some sweets.
Then beneath moonbeam trees,
They drank blue fruit juice and
Munched moon-made cream cheese.

They got back in the Moonsnoop
And took off from the moon.
'Thank you,' said Susan.
'We'll both come back soon!'